Suffer Well

Endure necessary suffering
in order to avoid
unnecessary suffering

LANDRY TIENTCHEU

BALBOA.PRESS

A DIVISION OF HAY HOUSE

Balboa Press books may be ordered through booksellers or by contacting:

Balboa Press
A Division of Hay House
1663 Liberty Drive
Bloomington, IN 47403
www.balboapress.com
844-682-1282

Because of the dynamic nature of the Internet, any web addresses or links contained in this book may have changed since publication and may no longer be valid. The views expressed in this work are solely those of the author and do not necessarily reflect the views of the publisher, and the publisher hereby disclaims any responsibility for them.

The author of this book does not dispense medical advice or prescribe the use of any technique as a form of treatment for physical, emotional, or medical problems without the advice of a physician, either directly or indirectly. The intent of the author is only to offer information of a general nature to help you in your quest for emotional and spiritual well-being. In the event you use any of the information in this book for yourself, which is your constitutional right, the author and the publisher assume no responsibility for your actions.

Any people depicted in stock imagery provided by Getty Images are models, and such images are being used for illustrative purposes only. Certain stock imagery © Getty Images.

Interior Image Credit: Awais Nawaz

Print information available on the last page.

ISBN: 978-1-9822-6947-0 (sc)
ISBN: 978-1-9822-6949-4 (hc)
ISBN: 978-1-9822-6948-7 (e)

Library of Congress Control Number: 2021910660

Balboa Press rev. date: 07/01/2021

Contents

Dedication

I dedicate this collection of wisdom to my suffering alter ego, who's taught me that hard is good.

Supplication

———— ⌘ ————

I pray for hardship so I can finally transcend my wicked ways.

Life

---◦◦◦---

Life is the ultimate dictator.
Either I have reverence for it, or it will crush me.

Initiation

To be an adult, I must be initiated.
To be initiated, I must suffer well.
To suffer well, I must endure.
To endure, I must never pass on my woe.
Instead, I shall transmute my pain into gold.
The gold of virtuous adulthood shall be my legacy.

Legacy

The habits I pass on will go much further than any tangible asset I leave behind, including knowledge.

Entitlement

I'm not entitled to a healthy body.
I'm not entitled to a healthy relationship.
I'm not entitled to the honesty of others.
I'm not entitled to the kindness of others.
I'm not entitled to live in a prosperous nation.
I'm not entitled to punish others because I have suffered.
I'm entitled to none of that.

The only thing I'm entitled to is the intrinsic reward of sharing the gift of my life with others.

Life owes me nothing. I, on the other hand, owe life my very best.

The Meaning of Life

———— ✑ ————

Life is a blank slate.
I give it meaning by the choices I make.
Meaning is a psychological experience, not a factual one.

My Purpose

I am Life. And that's all the purpose there is.

When Life calls me to be still, I am still.
When Life calls me to serve it, I do it with gusto.

That's all there is to it.

Power

***

To acquire power, I must.
Not by hoarding, but by giving.
Not by enslaving, but by empowering.
Not by being the fittest, but by being the most conscious.
Not by consuming the power of others, but by yielding my own.

Power begets power.

Commitment

───────── ❧ ─────────

Love is cute, but commitment is reliable.
Friendship is nice, but commitment is useful.
Entrepreneurship is cool, but commitment builds.

Commitment animates universal principles. It makes God pay attention.

Sacrifice

I wish, but still.
I speak, but still.
I argue, but still.
I defend, but still.
I sacrifice, and yet.

Life rewards sacrifice, not positive affirmations.

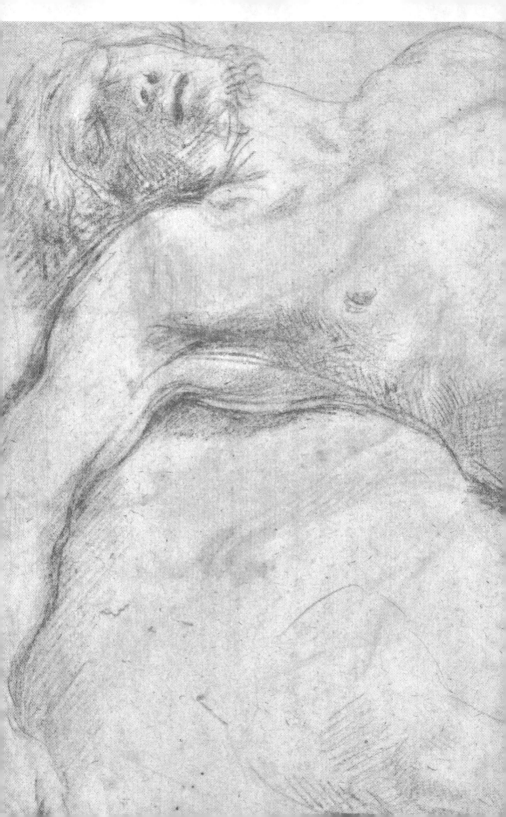

Motion

Either I get physical, or I get depressed.
There's no middle ground.
There's no ambiguity.
It's a choice.

Happiness

———— ✑ ————

I am happiest when I embrace the inevitable suffering of the human condition.

The Choice

I don't get to choose whether I will suffer. That part is not up to me. What's up to me is how well I will suffer when my time comes.

Trust

I only trust people who have suffered.
Their word is founded not upon illusions but upon reality.

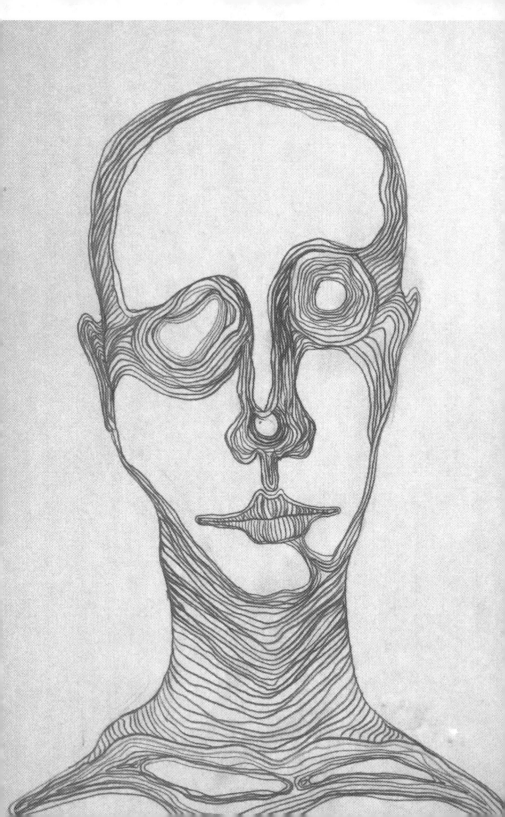

Evil

Evil is real. And the potential to perpetrate evil resides at the core of every single human being, regardless of how noble the packaging is.

I do make a deal with the devil...

When I'm in denial about its existence.
When I wait an eternity for my savior to come.
When I'm casual with people's heart in the name of sex.
When every single fiber of my being knows better.
When I settle for "It's Just Business."

Until I own that, it will seem an impossible feat to sever that allegiance.

Sin

It's no concern of mine if I hurt your ego.
But it is a significant concern of mine if I hurt your soul.

The soul is an instrument of service.
It's the instrument through which humanity achieves wholeness.

Every time I hurt your soul, I have sinned.

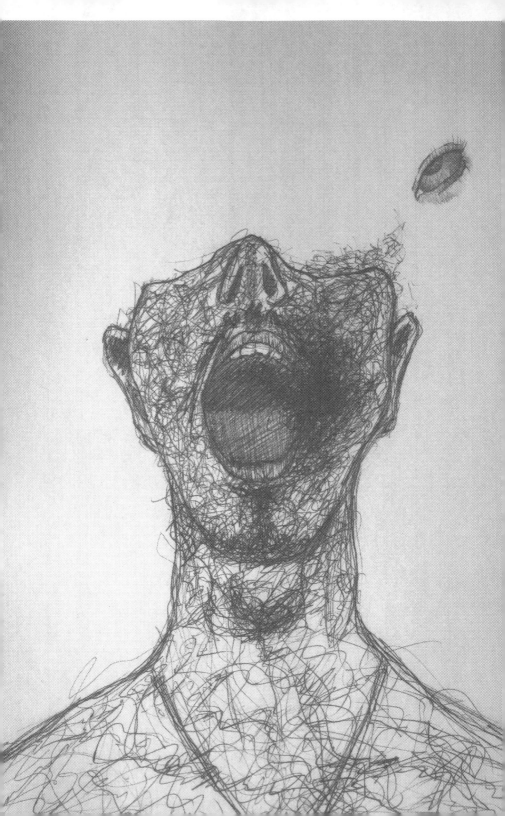

Jesus

No amount of Jesus's dying on the cross will save me.

To resurrect from my unwise choices, I must go through my own crucifixion. I may not lose my body in the process, but I will definitely lose my mind.

It's a price I alone have the privilege to pay.

Declaration of War

--- ❧ ---

Birth into this world is a declaration of war.

This world is designed to...
fill my body with junk,
fill my mind with filth, &
trap my spirit within illusions.

Why? To suppress my soul.
Why? Because my soul can move mountains with one word.

For anyone who knows anything, the human soul is the ultimate price
in this world.

Power emanates from the soul, not from what I have. This world will
let you have anything, but it will never let you be anything.

It takes a committed warrior indeed to overcome the ways of the world.

Blessed Enemy

--- ✑ ---

There's no Batman without Joker.
There's no James Bond without Spectre.
There's no Superman without Lex Luthor.

To achieve anything worthwhile, I need a worthy enemy, one who is just as committed to seeing me fail as I am to succeed.

Freedom

If I need much to get by, I'm a slave.
Freedom is getting by with very little.

Unanswered Prayer

An unanswered prayer is actually the answer to the prayer.
I'm not entitled to everything I ask, including peace in the world.
I don't get to call the shots. Life does.

Identity

I am God's desire to have a physical experience in the form of me, painful or otherwise.

Gift

The only gift of importance is that which transforms the recipient into a mustard seed capable of displacing the mountains of injustice. Such a paradigm shift can often be achieved when, in the words of Walter Benjamin, the gift affects the recipient to the point of shock.

As a creator, I find shock value is often the greatest gift to offer a world that has grown comfortable with sin. It's a very unpleasant endeavor for both the giver and the giftee. Yet, amid shock value, the potential to transform for the better "at light speed" is real, palpable, and humongous.

Death

Death is an ally.
It continually reminds me of the preciousness of now.
The sooner I make peace with it, the faster it will work on my behalf.

Forever

The fountain of youth doesn't exist.
The fountain of discipline, on the other hand, is everlasting.
If I drink from it, I can stick around and be useful for a little while longer.

The Void

If I live long enough, I will experience the existential void.
Food, alcohol, drugs, and sex will not fill it.

The void is normal, scheduled, and purposeful.
It is a portal for divine intervention.

I must feel it;
I must suffer its pain &
I must let God fill it up with my next life assignment.

Wholesome Sickness

Sickness is part of the healing process. If I don't permit myself to get sick, I also don't permit myself to heal. The two are inseparable.

The Cure

"All diseases are curable. But not all people are." —Irène Grosjean

Paradoxically, I become alive again when I make peace with my not having what it takes to heal.

Life rejoices in my being alive, not blaming the whole world for my incapacity to heal.

Rights

The right to always do right by others is my only right.

Adulting

It's very tempting to remain childish forever.
After all, growing up does come with limitations and responsibilities.

Yet life demands we sacrifice and suffer for the common good;
otherwise, there will be nothing left to be childish about.

I can only do that as an adult. I can be the steward of what's true and
everlasting about the human experience.

Self-Grooming

―――――――――――― ❧ ――――――――――――

I've been groomed to always look forward to spring and summer. Now it's time I learn to enjoy fall and winter without ever wishing them away.

Heartbreak

Thank you for breaking my heart open.
Now I can include "the other" in my circle of compassion.

The Purge

When suffering takes away everything but my willingness to love unconditionally, with one word, I shall heal the entire human race.

Divine Debt

My life is kept together by a set of laws cosmic in size, organic in nature, and nonnegotiable by design. One law is the law of cause and effect.

I don't get to participate in the cause of anything and then sit around and wonder where God is when I'm experiencing the effects. No!

What I get to say is: "All right! I now understand the rules of the game. And in honor of my great ancestor Maya Angelou, next time I'll do better."

The Least of Us

❧

What I do to the least of us, I do to all of us. This law is not exclusive to human beings. It applies to the galactic community, including all the offspring of Mother Earth.

When I forcefully harvest plants to extract their medicinal properties, I empower the harvesting of "lesser" humans to heal the wealthy among us. We call it human trafficking.

When I forcibly impregnate cows so I can drink the milk intended for calves, I empower nonconsensual sex among human beings for the sake of pleasure. We call it rape.

When I feed pigs junk to fatten them up to my liking, I empower the junk food industry designed to feed us, not nourish us. We call it a health crisis.

Whether or not I believe in the "the least of us" law is irrelevant. The law is at work with or without my consent. It is in my best interest to tread very carefully on this earth, remembering that how I do anything is how I do everything, and how I treat anyone is how I treat everyone.

UFOs

Any time I see another species, all I want to do is

- *hunt it*
- *kill it*
- *slaughter it*
- *eat it*
- *domesticate it*
- *pet it*
- *humanize it*
- *civilize it*
- *save it*
- *conquer it*
- *enslave it*
- *colonize it*
- *showcase it*
- *worship it*
- *study it*
- *teach it*
- *master it*
- *dominate it*
- *control it*
- *exploit it*
- *industrialize it*
- *commercialize it*
- *sell it*
- *etc.*

Then I turn around and wonder why UFOs are so distant and unfriendly.

Safety Net

--- ❦ ---

Insurance policies are business deals that can only be sustained in times of prosperity. Generosity, on the other hand, is part of the covenant God made with humans; it's an insurance policy that transcends space and time.

When all systems fail, how generous I am will always be a reliable safety net. The human spirit is wired to provide safety to those who have been generous of heart.

Born Equal

---- ❦ ----

Empires are notorious for spreading the idea that we're all born equal. It's an excellent marketing slogan, but it's not true. Such a belief leads to two types of behaviors:

- **Either I spend my life trying to fit in;**
- **Or I spend it preaching my lifestyle to others.**

That's the perfect recipe for slavery, which empires thrive on.

Don't seek equality. Seek sovereignty.

A sovereign mind dissolves the empire.
A sovereign mind becomes its own empire.

Free Will

─────── ⟶ ───────

As long as I'm willing to live the consequences of my choices, what I say goes. No government, no army, no religious cult, no ET, no invisible spirits, not even God can stand in the way of my free will when I decide with conviction this is how it will be.

My choice to sin and suffer the consequences is as legal in God's eyes as is my choice to do the right thing and reap the rewards. God loves me enough to honor both choices.

Recipe for Life

———— ✺ ————

My mind is the soil.
My deeds are the seeds.
My thoughts, ideas, and perceptions are the fruits.

No matter what my reality suggests, through repeated actions enhanced
by selected words, I always have the agency to seed a brand-new world.

With...
one cup of suffering,
one pound of practice,
half a cup of perseverance,
and a zest of patience,

this brand-new world shall come to pass. It's bound to.

Highest Potential

My highest potential is revealed when I can witness the suffering of my mind in silence.

Sanity

The secret to my sanity is that...
...I don't believe everything that goes through my mind.

Thoughtxicity

❦

Thoughtxicity is the process through which I pollute the psychic air by verbalizing unhealthy thoughts.

When a thought bangs at the door of my psyche, I immediately recognize it as unhealthy. A healthy thought will never force itself onto me. It will come around sometimes (or every now and then, depending on how relevant its blessing is), but it respects one of the fundamental laws of this universe: free will. It understands that all it can do is offer, but that choice is always mine.

When on the other hand, a thought is persistent enough to give me headaches, there's always a hidden agenda at work, usually a dark one, no matter how innocent or rational that thought might look. If I verbalize it to get some relief, I have become a co-creator in this dark agenda. Furthermore, if I verbalize it in the presence of other people, I have empowered that thought to recruit more minds and grow more powerful, thus turning into a thought form. Eventually, if all those newly recruited minds verbalize it as well, the thought form grows into a powerful egregore that can then bend the laws of our world and corrupt common sense to justify its existence. It becomes a psychic entity that unleashes hell on earth through our own allegiance.

I must suffer through the headaches of banging thoughts if I want to lessen my karmic load and that of my fellow human beings. Sooner or later, once a dark thought realizes that I can see it for what it is and not speak it, it'll move on and harass someone else. If enough human beings choose not to empower it, it will dissolve.

Meditation

The more I meditate,
the more I can witness my thoughts.

The more I witness my thoughts,
the wider the gap is between thought and expression.

The longer I reside between thought and expression,
the less triggered I am.

The more I transcend my triggers,
the freer I become.

Love

---⌘---

I love you when I fall in or out of love.
I love you when I succeed or fail.
I love you when I love or hate.
I love you when I build or destroy.
I love you when I'm kind or mean.
I love you beyond my polarities.

"Love is a commitment to a person, not to that person's behavior."
—Seth Godin

"Love Myself"

***

I've been loving myself a little too much lately, and the whole planet is suffering because of that. If I can't balance loving myself with loving others, I'll always be off track.

Relationship Course

———— ❧ ————

Life is, first and foremost, a relationship course.

I'm not here to figure out how to go to the moon. That's just a hobby.

I'm here primarily to master the art of doing human relationships well. That's nonnegotiable.

I can bypass that assignment all I want. The assignment, however, will not bypass me. Sooner or later, I must take the course.

Scarcity

———— ✌ ————

True love lives in the land of scarcity.

Before the power of love is made mine, the god of scarcity will act on behalf of love to strip away from me all the junk I cherish so much.

Eternal Flesh

✧

I always run away from anyone that sells eternal flesh.

Why? Because by its very design, nature always aborts the life of its most voracious consumers to sustain itself.

Suicide

First, I must find out what makes me come alive.
Then, I must be courageous enough to let it kill me.

Creation: The Ultimate Power

———— ∽ ————

"What we design designs us back." —Jason Silva

Any creation puts a dent in the universe. Through the law of cause and effect, what I create sets in motion ripple effects that affect not only me but the entire cosmos.

If I want to transform humanity, I have only to create something powerful enough to transform the one.

The New Covenant

I pray that I suffer enough to realize that I should never, ever pass on my suffering but my healing.

Printed in the United States
by Baker & Taylor Publisher Services